STYLE YOUR *MIND*

A Workbook and Lifestyle Guide for Women
Who Want to Design Their Thoughts,
Empower Themselves, and
Build a Beautiful Life

FROM AMAZON BESTSELLING AUTHOR
CARA ALWILL LEYBA

About this Experience

Style Your Mind is a workbook and lifestyle guide for women who wish to make personal and professional changes using the life coaching process. Filled with powerful questions, thought-provoking activities, inspirational quotes, and lifestyle tips, master life coach and best selling personal development author Cara Alwill Leyba leads you on a journey to style your mind, empower yourself, and ultimately live your most gorgeous life.

STYLE YOUR *MIND*

Cover and interior design by Ryan Leyba
Photography by Angelica Glass

ISBN-13: 978-0-692-83755-9

For more, visit www.CaraAlwill.com
or email Info@CaraAlwill.com

Table of Contents

"You can't change your life by doing the *same things* every day."

– CARA ALWILL LEYBA
#STYLEYOURMIND

Hello Gorgeous!

First, I'd like to congratulate you on choosing yourself. By investing in this experience, you've sent a powerful message to the universe that you are committed doing the thrilling and challenging work of thinking and living better.

I am so honored that you've selected me as your guide through this transformative time of your life. As a master life coach and author of five bestselling personal development books, nothing inspires me more than watching someone evolve into the person they are meant to be.

Throughout my career, I have worked with thousands of women and been a witness to rebirths, reinventions, and complete lifestyle and mindset makeovers. It's truly astonishing what we can do when we realize we are capable of changing our own lives. When we realize that no one is to blame, and that we are responsible for deciding what we desire, and then going out into the world to claim it.

Within the pages of this guide, you'll find a series of mindset shifts, affirming mantras, powerful questions, success rituals, and thought-provoking exercises to help you style your mind and design your life. I encourage you to take your time with this experience. Know that you can come back to this practice at any point in time – even after you complete it. These tools will stand the test of time, and you'll be surprised at how often you'll want to check in with yourself and revisit these pages.

And, as a very special bonus, I've included a 30-day journaling experience packed with cues and inspiring quotes called *Style Your Day*, where you'll have a chance to reflect and write down whatever you'd like. Feel free to complete this before, during, or after your workbook.

So take a deep breath, light a candle, and begin.

With love, fire, and intention,

Cara

"Your past is gone.
Your mistakes are behind you.
Focus on your gorgeous, love-filled *future*. The only thing you are responsible for now is taking each step with intention.
Rebuild your life.
Make it *gold*."

– CARA ALWILL LEYBA
#STYLEYOURMIND

What is Life Coaching?

Life coaching is the process of empowering an individual to reach within and remove their own blocks, overcome obstacles, and live and think better. In a traditional life coaching relationship, a professionally trained coach works closely with their client to fulfill the client's objectives. A coach can help you identify your blind spots, ask you questions you may not have asked yourself, and hold you accountable to your goals.

Life coaches are non-judgmental and non-critical, and will guide you through the process of self-discovery and self-improvement in a way that your family or friends may be incapable of.

Life coaching is always focused on the present and the future, and rarely the past. The process is about moving forward and recognizing that you are responsible for making your life as wonderful as you can imagine it to be.

CARA'S CERTIFICATION AND CREDENTIALS

Cara Alwill Leyba is a certified master life coach, and obtained her training through the ICF-accredited World Coach Institute. Cara holds two niche certifications in both life and wellness coaching, and has worked with women around the world through her private programs, group workshops, and events. She is the author of five bestselling personal development books, and her work has appeared in magazines like *Glamour*, *Shape*, *Marie Claire*, *Success*, *The Huffington Post*, and others, as well as on broadcast programs around the country. Cara's full bio can be found in the back of this workbook.

The Power of the Question

When I first began studying life coaching, I was amazed at how effective asking questions can be. There is something dynamic that happens when we empower others to find the answers within themselves, rather than giving advice. By presenting questions, sometimes profound, yet sometimes, very simple, we allow the other person the opportunity to pause and reflect, and ultimately, arrive at the place they need to be. And that is the true essence of life coaching.

As I stepped into my field and began asking my clients about things like their mindset, their challenges, and their thought patterns, it occurred to me that I had never even asked myself some of these things!

As years went on, and I began working with more and more women, I was astounded by how far we could get in a coaching session just by posing a few questions they had never thought about before. I watched my clients bloom and become the best versions of themselves by becoming self-aware. I not only use the questions in this workbook with my clients, but I use them in my own life, as well. And the best part? You can come back to these pages at any time. I have personally been revisiting some of these very questions for years now, and the answers surprise and enlighten me each time.

Throughout each section of this workbook, I will ask you a series of things that will help you reflect on each area of your life. I encourage you to create a serene and inspiring environment, free of clutter and distraction when you answer them. Light a candle, pour a cup of tea, and put on some relaxing music. Give yourself the gift of time and focus to dedicate to these pages.

And please remember, there are no right or wrong answers. All I ask is that you allow your honesty and intuition to guide you.

"Do not apologize for your decision to *elevate* your thoughts, *upgrade* your standards, or separate yourself from those who interrupt your *greatness*."

– CARA ALWILL LEYBA
#STYLEYOURMIND

Creating Your Vision

First thing's first. It's time to create a vision for yourself. Without an overarching picture of how you'd like your life to look, its impossible to build goals to get there. In the space below, write the story of who you are in your ideal world. Don't be afraid to dream big, and be as detailed as possible. Please leave out specific goals (ex: lose 10 pounds in one month), but instead, think about the bigger vision.

Here are a few prompts to get you started:

What kind of woman are you?

Where do you live?

What do you do for a living?

How do you dress?

How do you make others feel?

IN THE SPACE BELOW, AND ON THE NEXT PAGE, WRITE OUT YOUR VISION:

_____

_____

_____

_____

_____

_____

_____

_____

_____

_____

_____

_____

_____

_____

_____

_____

_____

_____

_____

_____

_____

_____

_____

_____

_____

_____

_____

_____

_____

_____

_____

_____

"Be *flexible*, but not desperate.
Be *humble*, yet confident.
Be open-minded,
yet *focused* on your vision."

– CARA ALWILL LEYBA
#STYLEYOURMIND

Defining Success

If you were to line up ten women in a room and ask them to define "success," I can bet my Chanel 2.55 jumbo caviar flap bag they'd all have a totally different answer. To some, success is making a million dollars and traveling the world. To others, success is staying home and raising a family. And to others, success is having a decent job and paying their bills on time.

Its important to define success on your *own terms* in order live a happy life. So many of us get caught up in how others define success, and we base our goals and accomplishments against that standard. If you've ever felt yourself going through the motions and doing something you truly didn't want to do, then you know exactly what I'm talking about.

The following exercises and questions will help you begin to uncover your own core beliefs, values, and ideas around success. Take your time with them, and try to let go of any limiting beliefs you may have around your own capabilities.

WHAT DOES SUCCESS MEAN TO YOU?

_____

_____

_____

_____

_____

_____

_____

_____

_____

_____

WHERE DID YOU LEARN THIS DEFINITION?

_____

_____

_____

_____

_____

_____

_____

_____

ARE YOU SUCCESSFUL?

_____

_____

_____

_____

_____

_____

_____

_____

_____

WHY?

_____

_____

_____

_____

_____

_____

_____

_____

_____

IF NOT, WHAT WOULD IT TAKE FOR YOU TO GET THERE?

_____

_____

_____

_____

_____

_____

_____

_____

WHEN HAVE YOU FELT SUCCESSFUL IN THE PAST?

_____

_____

_____

_____

_____

_____

_____

_____

WHAT LED TO THAT SUCCESS?

_____

_____

_____

_____

_____

_____

_____

_____

WHO WERE YOU WHEN THAT SUCCESS HAPPENED?

_____

_____

_____

_____

_____

_____

_____

_____

WHO HELPED YOU WIN?

_____

_____

_____

_____

_____

_____

_____

_____

_____

WHO ARE SOME SUCCESSFUL PEOPLE YOU ADMIRE?

_____

_____

_____

_____

_____

_____

_____

_____

WHAT ARE THE QUALITIES ABOUT THOSE PEOPLE THAT YOU LIKE?

_____

_____

_____

_____

_____

_____

_____

_____

_____

_____

Future Success

WHAT IS ONE AREA OF YOUR LIFE YOU'D LIKE TO BE SUCCESSFUL IN?

_____

_____

_____

_____

_____

_____

_____

WHAT WILL IT TAKE TO GET YOU THERE?

_____

_____

_____

_____

_____

_____

_____

_____

_____

WHAT QUALITIES, SKILLS, AND TALENTS DO YOU HAVE NOW THAT WILL HELP YOU BE SUCCESSFUL?

_____

_____

_____

_____

_____

_____

_____

WHAT NEW SKILLS DO YOU NEED TO ACQUIRE?

_____

_____

_____

_____

_____

_____

_____

WHAT ELSE CAN YOU LEARN?

_____

_____

_____

_____

_____

_____

_____

_____

_____

WHAT DO YOU NEED TO LEAVE IN THE PAST?

_____

_____

_____

_____

_____

_____

_____

_____

_____

WRITE A PERSONAL MANTRA ABOUT SUCCESS

"And then there is the turning point. The place where you become *intimate* with your intuition. Where you realize other people's input can be valuable, but it is never *vital.* Where you are no longer afraid to make the call, to have the final say, and to become the CEO of your *universe.*"

– CARA ALWILL LEYBA
#STYLEYOURMIND

Celebrating Your Strengths

We all have talents and qualities that help us win. And often times, we focus so much on what we don't have, that we neglect to celebrate what we do. When we choose to celebrate the good, we reprogram our minds. That simple shift can guarantee us more success and more confidence, and ultimately, a better life.

The next few questions will help you identify your strengths so you can build your confidence and learn to rock what you've got!

WHAT IS YOUR BEST QUALITY?

_____

_____

_____

_____

_____

_____

_____

_____

_____

_____

_____

_____

_____

WHAT DO YOU LOVE MOST ABOUT YOURSELF?

_____

_____

_____

_____

_____

_____

_____

_____

WHAT'S GREAT ABOUT YOUR LIFE?

_____

_____

_____

_____

_____

_____

_____

_____

_____

WHAT WOULD YOUR CLOSEST FRIENDS SAY ABOUT YOU?

_____

_____

_____

_____

_____

_____

_____

_____

WHAT AREA OF YOUR LIFE DO YOU FEEL MOST ALIGNED WITH?

_____

_____

_____

_____

_____

_____

_____

_____

_____

WHAT IS YOUR BIGGEST TALENT?

_____

_____

_____

_____

_____

_____

_____

WHAT GIVES YOU ENERGY?

_____

_____

_____

_____

_____

_____

_____

_____

WHAT ARE YOU PASSIONATE ABOUT?

_____

_____

_____

_____

_____

_____

_____

_____

WHAT MAKES YOU FEEL ALIVE?

_____

_____

_____

_____

_____

_____

_____

_____

_____

_____

"You will do your best work when you stop looking around and start looking *within*."

– CARA ALWILL LEYBA
#STYLEYOURMIND

Identifying Your Blocks

We all have things that hold us back. Let's identify those blocks so we can start to move past them. Remember: the sooner you know what is keeping you stuck, the sooner you can become unstuck!

WHAT HOLDS YOU BACK?

_____

_____

_____

_____

_____

_____

_____

_____

_____

_____

_____

_____

_____

_____

_____

_____

_____

_____

WHAT IS SOMETHING YOU REALLY WANT TO ACCOMPLISH, BUT FEEL BLOCKED?

_____

_____

_____

_____

_____

_____

_____

_____

WHAT HAVE YOU GIVEN UP ON?

_____

_____

_____

_____

_____

_____

_____

_____

WHY DO YOU THINK YOU'VE GIVEN UP?

_____
_____
_____
_____
_____
_____
_____
_____

WHAT ARE YOU AFRAID OF?

_____
_____
_____
_____
_____
_____
_____
_____

WHAT DRAINS YOU?

_____
_____
_____
_____
_____
_____
_____
_____

WHAT AREAS OF YOUR LIFE FEEL STRESSFUL OR UNBALANCED?

_____
_____
_____
_____
_____
_____
_____
_____
_____

HOW WOULD YOUR LIFE CHANGE IF YOU BECAME UNSTUCK?

Dream Design:
Goals, Timelines, and Accountability

By this point, you've done some serious work on creating your vision, identifying your blocks, and celebrating your strengths. Congratulations! You have built a solid foundation for designing your goals and ultimately changing your life. Take a moment to celebrate the work you've done thus far. Pour yourself a glass of champagne (or sparkling water in a pretty glass!) and toast yourself. You deserve it.

Now it's time to create a strategy. Having a vision is crucial, but without designing clear goals to hold yourself accountable to, it means nothing. As the saying goes, "the dream is free, but the hustle is sold separately."

Over the next few pages, we'll dig in and start drawing up a serious game plan for you to start making things happen.

Refer back to your vision. What are the top 3 things that need to happen in order to start making that vision a reality?

GOAL 1:

_____

_____

_____

_____

_____

_____

_____

_____

_____

GOAL 2:

_____

_____

_____

_____

_____

_____

_____

_____

GOAL 3:

_____

_____

_____

_____

_____

_____

_____

_____

_____

GOAL 1

Action Step 1: _____

To be completed by: _____

Action Step 2: _____

To be completed by: _____

Action Step 3: _____

To be completed by: _____

GOAL 2

Action Step 1: _____

To be completed by: _____

Action Step 2: _____

To be completed by: _____

Action Step 3: _____

To be completed by: _____

GOAL 3

Action Step 1: _____

To be completed by: _____

Action Step 2: _____

To be completed by: _____

Action Step 3: _____

To be completed by: _____

Accountability

Studies show that we're more willing to stick to our goals and promises if we tell someone about them. I recommend finding a success partner to help you stay on track and motivate you when you need it. Whether it's your spouse, your best friend, your mom, or one of your Facebook friends, try to share your plan with someone else, and offer to be their accountability partner as well.

If you can't find someone else to keep you accountable, or you'd rather keep your goals private, set an alarm on your phone with your completion date, and the days leading up to it, to stay motivated.

LIST YOUR ACCOUNTABILITY PARTNER BELOW AND HOW OFTEN YOU WILL CHECK IN WITH THEM:

_____

_____

_____

_____

_____

_____

_____

_____

_____

_____

"Do *not* leave this world with books, plans, or words *inside* of you."

– CARA ALWILL LEYBA
#STYLEYOURMIND

Mindset Magic

It's impossible to truly live your best life without a proper mindset. A mindset that supports the idea that you deserve to be happy, successful, abundant, and loved. A mindset that recognizes fear, but moves forward intelligently and strategically to chase dreams regardless. A mindset that sees rejection as opportunity to reposition. A mindset that believes you are worthy of your wildest desires.

HOW DOES YOUR CURRENT MINDSET HELP YOU SUCCEED?

WHAT WOULD YOU LIKE TO CHANGE ABOUT YOUR MINDSET?

_____

_____

_____

_____

_____

_____

_____

_____

WRITE DOWN 3 POSITIVE THOUGHTS THAT WILL HELP YOU
LIVE YOUR BEST LIFE:

_____

_____

_____

_____

_____

_____

_____

_____

_____

Talk is Chic

WHAT ARE SOME OF THE THINGS YOU SAY TO YOURSELF ON A REGULAR BASIS?

_____

_____

_____

_____

_____

_____

_____

_____

HOW DO THEY MAKE YOU FEEL?

_____

_____

_____

_____

_____

_____

_____

_____

DO YOU SPEAK HIGHLY OF YOURSELF?

_____

_____

_____

_____

_____

_____

_____

_____

_____

HOW CAN YOU BE KINDER TO YOURSELF?

_____

_____

_____

_____

_____

_____

_____

_____

IF YOU SPOKE TO YOURSELF THE WAY YOU SPEAK TO YOUR BEST FRIEND, HOW WOULD LIFE CHANGE?

Self-Compassion

It's important to realize that we all make mistakes from time to time, and the faster your forgive yourself, the happier you will be. This is not an excuse to be reckless with yourself or others, but you need to learn to practice self-compassion and move on after a mishap.

Maybe you flubbed a presentation at work, or had a little too much to drink at a party and said something you're embarrassed by, but you've got to let it go.

WRITE DOWN A LIST OF THINGS YOU WILL COMMIT TO FORGIVING YOURSELF FOR:

_____

_____

_____

_____

_____

_____

_____

_____

_____

_____

_____

_____

_____

_____

_____

_____

Abundance & Possibilities

Do you believe you are capable of achieving the goals you set? Do you truly feel that you deserve to live the life you wrote about in your vision? These are serious questions that deserve serious reflection. Unless you believe that your possibilities are unlimited, and that your life can be as big and bold and beautiful as you wish it to be, you'll find yourself stuck.

Below are some mantras to help you feel more abundant and limitless:

I am brilliantly powerful.

The world needs me and my unique gifts.

My possibilities are unlimited and success and happiness flow easily to me.

I am a magnet for wonderful opportunities.

What is meant for me will not pass me.

IN THE SPACE BELOW, WRITE YOUR OWN ABUNDANCE MANTRAS:

_____

_____

_____

_____

_____

_____

_____

_____

_____

"Cling to your hunger. Find your stride inside of it. And never be ashamed of your *aching* for something more."

– CARA ALWILL LEYBA
#STYLEYOURMIND

Gorgeously Grateful

Gratitude is one of the quickest ways to change your life. By focusing on what we're grateful for, we attract more into our worlds, and ultimately, become happier, more peaceful women.

In fact, studies show that practice gratitude can also improve our health. According to a 2012 study published in *Personality and Individual Differences*, grateful people report experiencing fewer aches and pains and feeling healthier overall. Grateful people are also more inclined to exercise regularly and maintain their health by visiting doctors and taking care of themselves.

And it's not just physical health that is improved by gratitude. Robert A. Emmons, Ph.D., one of the world's leading gratitude researchers, has conducted multiple studies on the link between gratitude and wellbeing. His research confirms that gratitude reduces depression and increases happiness.

I recommend creating a gratitude practice and infusing it into your every day. I personally practice gratitude at night before going to sleep, and in the morning upon waking, by thinking of five things I am thankful for. Truth be told, I usually wind up listing at least ten or twenty!

IN THE SPACE BELOW, WRITE DOWN FIVE THINGS YOU ARE THANKFUL FOR:

_____

_____

_____

_____

_____

_____

_____

_____

_____

_____

_____

_____

_____

_____

_____

WRITE A PERSONAL GRATITUDE MANTRA TO HELP CENTER YOU AND HELP YOU DEAL WITH FEELINGS OF STRESS OR ANXIETY

_____

_____

_____

_____

_____

_____

_____

_____

_____

STYLE
YOUR
LIFE

Succcess Rituals and Lifestyle Tips
for Better Living

Little Luxuries:
6 Ways to Elevate Your Environment and Raise Your Glam Vibration

Styling your mind is not just about your personal development, it's also about creating a beautiful environment and nourishing rituals to support your new mindset. Whether its your home, your car, or your office, its crucial that you curate the world around you to reflect the way you want to feel inside. For me personally, my space must feel glam, feminine, and clean.

Over the years, I've developed go-to rituals and must-haves in my home that help nurture my mind, body, and soul. And the best part? You don't need to invest thousands of dollars to make your life feel luxurious. Here are my 6 tried-and-true ways to elevate your environment and raise your *glam vibration*:

SUBSCRIBE TO A HOME DELIVERY OF YOUR FAVORITE NEWSPAPER

Ever turn on the news in the morning and immediately feel anxious? Between the drama, the debating "experts," and the commercials, watching the morning news can be toxic. I cut out television in the mornings years ago and it has transformed my world. I subscribe to the New York Times home delivery and receive my news that way. I light a candle, savor my coffee, and catch up what's going on in the world on my terms, without all the noise.

CURATE A BEAUTIFUL COFFEE MUG COLLECTION

It may seem small, but drinking your coffee out of a pretty mug makes all the difference. I am head over heels for vintage tea cups, and I also love mugs with positive quotes and affirmations.

PURCHASE UNIFORM HANGERS FOR YOUR CLOSET

I recently created a capsule wardrobe, and it has shifted me in a way I could never have imagined. One of my favorite aspects of my new closet is the fact that my hangers are now all uniform. I am obsessed with black velvet hangers. They make everything look sleek, and I feel like I'm shopping in a boutique every time I pick out my outfits.

USE AN AROMATHERAPY DIFFUSER

Want your home to instantly smell like a spa? Buy an aromatherapy diffuser and use it with your favorite essentials oils. Eucalyptus is my absolute favorite. I fire it up every morning and it energizes me and makes me feel like I'm working from a 5-star hotel. You can choose whatever aromas work for you: lavender, peppermint, the list goes on. Research the benefits of essential oils and go to town.

INVEST IN LUXURIOUS PAJAMAS

If there is one thing I love, it's luxe loungewear. I don't know about you, but I'm one of those people who get home and immediately change into comfy clothes. I will admit, I was having a love affair with sweats for a while, but I have since upgraded to a few delicious silk pajama sets and I've never looked back. They are soft and glam and look great whether you're wearing them to bed or just as your Saturday outfit.

USE PRETTY PENS AND STATIONARY

I'm big on writing lists. Lists of goals, dreams, things I'm celebrating, etc. And there is no better way to upgrade that practice than by using pretty pens and stationary. You can shop brands like Kate Spade for a bit of an elevated collection, or places like Home Goods which have some fantastic note pads at great prices.

Finding Inspiration:
6 Things to Do When You Feel Stuck

Inspiration: That elusive, magical, addictive, powerful force we all crave. The secret sauce to our most successful projects. When you've got it, you feel unstoppable. And when it's gone, well, it's gone.

I always ask my clients what they struggle with most, and this topic consistently comes up. Everyone wants to know how to get (and stay) inspired. I created a list of ways I find and keep inspiration in my own life, in the hopes that they may help you, too. One little caveat: I think inspiration is very personal. We all get fired up by different things, so please don't take this as an end-all, be-all list. Ask your soul what it needs on a regular basis, and give yourself that gift. And if you're craving some new ideas, here are mine:

STOP TRYING TO GET INSPIRED

This may sound totally counter-productive, but I find the more I try to force a feeling, the more it eludes me. If you're racking your brain trying to figure out why you can't get inspired, all you'll wind up doing is racking your brain. Put it out of your head and go do something else.

HELP SOMEONE ELSE

If you're stuck on finding your own inspiration, helping someone else find theirs can work for you, too. Focusing on another person's projects can help stir up ideas for yourself. It allows us to take the stress off our own thoughts and aids as a creative distraction. This has worked for me more times than I can count. And even if it doesn't help you, you can be happy knowing you've lifted someone else up. What's better than that?

GO LIVE YOUR LIFE

Most of the time when we're feeling uninspired, we're staring at a screen. I know I get into modes where I desperately try to find inspiration by clicking around on the web for hours. I somehow think an image on Pinterest or a quote on Instagram will spark something magical within me. But in reality, getting outside and living life is what will do it. Try taking a walk around your city with your headphones on, sitting outside and reading a book, or meeting up with your friends for an afternoon glass of wine. I always find myself inspired after great conversation or finding a piece of artwork on a New York City sidewalk.

MEDITATE

Do you know how slow and buggy your laptop gets when you don't reboot it for a few weeks? It starts loading web pages super slowly, and everything feels clouded. Our minds are the same. We need to "reboot" our brains regularly to dump out negative thoughts and old ideas to make room for the new. I'm no pro at meditation, but here's how I make it work for me: I sit up straight in a quiet space, and take a few deep cleansing breaths. Then, I get an image or mantra into my mind that I want to focus on. For example, if I'm meditating on getting inspired, I envision myself sitting at my computer, typing with abandon, candles burning all around me, feeling "in flow." I try to get lost in this feeling, as if its happening in the moment. As I inhale, I hold that visual in my mind. As I exhale, I let go of any fear, stress, or anxiety I have. I literally breathe out the bad thoughts. I repeat this for about 5 minutes and then get back to work.

WORK OUT

SoulCycle has been a game-changer for me. 45 minutes on a bike that goes nowhere allows my mind to go everywhere. I have had so many "a ha" moments during class it's truly amazing. Between the dark, candlelit room, the music, and the inspiring words from my instructor that seem to come out just when I need them, my time at Soul always leaves me refreshed, recharged, and ready to create. You don't have to do SoulCycle, but find something similar where you can really lose yourself. Go for a run and listen to music, or take a dance class. You'll also release endorphins during your workout, which does wonders for your brain chemistry and makes you feel happier and more creative, too.

REVAMP YOUR WORK SPACE

Whenever I feel blah, I switch up my workspace to make it feel more inviting. A few quick and inexpensive ways to do this are buying yourself fresh flowers and getting a few new scented candles. Depending on my budget, I'll pick up anything from a gorgeous, custom bouquet from my florist (I love monochromatic bouquets like all white), and a pre-made bouquet from the supermarket for $10 works wonders as well. I'll even drink my coffee from a beautiful vintage tea cup to make the experience feel more elegant. There is something about working in a pretty space that makes me feel instantly inspired.

Self-Love is a Verb:
How to Feel Confident and Get Your Groove Back

I don't think I've met one woman who doesn't struggle with the concept of self-love. If you've ever beat yourself up over the way you look, allowed yourself to be treated poorly by someone else, or doubted your worth, then you know what I'm talking about. The good news is, however your lack of self-love affects you, there are ways to work on it and develop a healthy, loving relationship with yourself. There are strategies and techniques to manage our anxiety and take off some of these heavy, heavy loads we wear on our backs. It is possible to learn to truly love yourself, to feel deserving, and style your mind in a way that serves your higher good.

WHEN IN DOUBT, JOURNAL IT OUT

My first go-to when I'm feeling anxious is free writing. Free writing is an exercise where you write the thoughts that come into your mind as they flow through you. There is no format, no judgment, and no rules. You simply document what you're thinking and let it all take shape. I find I uncover so much when I set aside 20-30 minutes to do this. I light a candle, pour a glass of wine, and set up a quiet environment that allows me to fully let go and release whatever is brewing in my mind. It not only helps me get to the bottom of my own stuff, it also helps spark creative ideas for the future. Total win/win.

CHECK IN ON YOUR SELF-CARE

This may be the most important thing on this list. Our minds and bodies are undeniably intertwined, and I know whenever I'm feeling badly about myself, 99% of the time I am treating my body poorly. I'm either not eating well, drinking too much wine, not taking enough hot baths, not getting regular massages, not working out, or not getting good sleep. All of this leads me to feel less confident, and self-love feels like the most foreign concept ever. If you can relate, its time to do an honest reality check on your wellness and then start making small changes. Plan some healthy meals you can cook yourself, start drinking more water with lemon, book a massage, or spend a few nights at home pampering yourself. Spend time connecting with your body by nourishing it with the right things and you will begin to feel better almost immediately I can usually lift my spirits within just 24 hours of a major self-care marathon.

GET THAT BODY IN MOTION

Book a workout class, go for a power walk, or just dance around your apartment. Get those endorphins flowing – they're like an injection of happiness. Even if you feel like crap, throw on some workout clothes, steer clear of all mirrors if you're the type to judge yourself (I know I can be) and just sweat. Knowing you committed to a workout will give you an instant boost of confidence.

WRITE YOURSELF A LOVE LETTER

Before you roll your eyes, hear me out. This can be a bit of an awkward exercise at first, but it is so empowering once you get started. Get some pretty stationary and get in the groove by making a list of all the things you love about yourself. Then, start writing it out in full sentences to form a letter. Tell yourself how proud you are of all your accomplishments. Compliment yourself on what a kind and loving person you are. Remind yourself of all the good in your life. Even if this feels a little silly, it works. You can even frame your letter and put it on your desk so you can be reminded of your kind words each day.

TREAT YOURSELF TO SOMETHING PRETTY

Consider this your permission slip to indulge a little. Depending on your budget, go and splurge on something to make you feel beautiful. Whether it's a new, bold lipstick shade, a pair of shoes you've had your eye on, or a new outfit that makes you feel incredible, you deserve it. When we look good, we feel good. Raise your glam vibration and kick your confidence into high gear. You don't have to go broke, but you should allow yourself a little something every now and then. It's called retail therapy for a reason, after all!

LISTEN TO YOUR FAVORITE MUSIC

Music heals. I know this to be true for as long as I can remember. There have been times in my life where literally every single thing felt like it was in shambles, and the only thing that saved me was music. Make yourself a playlist that makes you feel good. Take a walk with your headphones on, or drive around in your car and get lost in song lyrics. No matter what is happening in my life, music is my one constant that is always there for me, and always helps me feel better. Lately I've been really feeling jazz, especially French jazz. I put it on, make myself an espresso, and write.

Feel Good Now:
19 Ways to Boost Your Mood (That Cost Nothing!)

One of the most common questions I get from women is, "How do I break out of a rut?" Life is constantly throwing us curve balls, presenting challenges, and testing our sanity. It's so easy to get wrapped up in a sea of stress and discontent, but there are also very powerful ways to battle those obstacles and not only keep your cool – but feel great despite what is happening around you.

While we'd all love to be able to book a weekend getaway to St. Barts or get a weekly massage at the Four Seasons, its not always possible financially. And honestly? Those things don't always do the trick. There are deeper, more powerful ways to feel good that go beyond material items. So I came up with 19 totally free ways to feel good now. And the best part is many of these things will also help someone else, too.

Perform a random act of kindness

Take a walk in nature without your phone

Sign up to volunteer for a cause that is important to you

Exercise (walk, run, hike outdoors, run up and down the stairs)

Take a hot bubble bath (add rose petals if you have flowers around!)

Call an old friend

Make a meal from scratch and eat it on your fanciest dish

Burn incense and make a wish

Get a small, meaningful tattoo with song lyrics or words you love

List 10 things you're thankful for

Make someone a playlist with songs that mean something to you

Wake up early and watch the sunrise

Reach out to someone to see if they need support/help

Make 3 meaningful promises to yourself

Write down all your fears and burn the list

Meditate

Write the first paragraph of the book you've always wanted to write

Make yourself a hot cup of tea with honey

Write a poem

Feel free to try any of my suggestions, or create your own list! Remember, we hold the keys to our mind. Be sure you are unlocking your best self, choosing your thoughts wisely, and always walking in your power. You've got this!

STYLE
YOUR
DAY

A 3o-Day Inspirational
and Reflective Journaling Experience

Day 1

SOME THINGS TO THINK ABOUT...

What gave you energy today?
What are you grateful for today?
How does gratitude change you as a person?

_____

_____

_____

_____

_____

_____

_____

_____

_____

_____

_____

_____

_____

_____

_____

_____

_____

"All we have is all we need. All we need is the awareness of how blessed we really are."
– Sarah Ban Breathnach

Day 2

SOME THINGS TO THINK ABOUT...

What excited you the most when you woke up today?
Did you believe in yourself today?
How can you believe in yourself more tomorrow?

_____

_____

_____

_____

_____

_____

_____

_____

_____

_____

_____

_____

_____

_____

"Believe in yourself and there will come a day when others will have no choice but to believe with you." – Cynthia Kersey

Day 5

What's the most fearless thing you did today?
How can you be more fearless tomorrow?
How does fear hold you back?

_____

_____

_____

_____

_____

_____

_____

_____

_____

_____

_____

_____

_____

_____

_____

_____

_____

_____

"Think like a queen. A queen is not afraid to fail. Failure is another steppingstone to greatness." – Oprah Winfrey

Day 4

SOME THINGS TO THINK ABOUT...

Did you feel successful today?
What does success mean to you?
How can you be more successful tomorrow?

_____

_____

_____

_____

_____

_____

_____

_____

_____

_____

_____

_____

_____

_____

_____

_____

"Success is liking yourself, liking what you do, and how you do it." – Maya Angelou

Day 5

SOME THINGS TO THINK ABOUT...

What negative thoughts hold you back?
What positive thoughts help you move forward?
How do you cultivate those positive thoughts?

"You need to learn how to select your thoughts just the same way you select your clothes every day. This is a power you can cultivate. If you want to control things in your life so bad, work on the mind. That's the only thing you should be trying to control." – Elizabeth Gilbert

Day 6

What was your major focus today?
What is something that you need to resolve?
What's keeping you from resolving it?

_____

_____

_____

_____

_____

_____

_____

_____

_____

_____

_____

_____

_____

_____

_____

_____

"If we did all the things we are capable of, we would literally astound ourselves." – Thomas Edison

Day 7

SOME THINGS TO THINK ABOUT...

How have you grown this week?
What did you learn?
What did you accomplish?

_____

_____

_____

_____

_____

_____

_____

_____

_____

_____

_____

_____

_____

_____

_____

"There is nothing like returning to a place that remains unchanged to find the ways in which you yourself have altered." – Nelson Mandela

Day 8

Did you enjoy the work you did today?

What is your dream job?

How can you start moving closer to your dream job this week?

_____

_____

_____

_____

_____

_____

_____

_____

_____

_____

_____

_____

_____

_____

"Your work is going to fill a large part of your life, and the only way to be truly satisfied is to do what you believe is great work. And the only way to do great work is to love what you do. If you haven't found it yet, keep looking. Don't settle. As with all matters of the heart, you'll know when you find it." – Steve Jobs

Day 9

SOME THINGS TO THINK ABOUT...

What could you be happy about if you chose to be?
What's stopping you from being happy?
In what areas did you feel limited today?

_____

_____

_____

_____

_____

_____

_____

_____

_____

_____

_____

_____

_____

_____

_____

_____

_____

"Follow your bliss and the universe will open doors where there were only walls." – Joseph Campbell

Day 10

SOME THINGS TO THINK ABOUT...

What do you value most in life?
Who do you value most in life?
Who values you?

_____

_____

_____

_____

_____

_____

_____

_____

_____

_____

_____

_____

_____

_____

_____

_____

"Decide the kind of woman you want to be, and go be her." – Unknown

Day 11

What is your biggest dream?
What is one thing you can do tomorrow that will bring you closer to it?
Do you believe you are worthy of this dream?

_____

_____

_____

_____

_____

_____

_____

_____

_____

_____

_____

_____

_____

_____

_____

_____

_____

"It is never too late to be what you might have been." – George Elliot

Day 12

SOME THINGS TO THINK ABOUT...

Do you have inner peace?
If not, how can you cultivate it?
How can you be more present?

_____

_____

_____

_____

_____

_____

_____

_____

_____

_____

_____

_____

_____

_____

_____

"Tomorrow has not invited you yet, so LIVE for today! Tomorrow is near, yet so far away. Choose this day to smile, laugh, love unconditionally, and be happy within." – Stephanie Lahart

Day 15

What are you passionate about?
How do you support that passion?
Who supports you?

_____

_____

_____

_____

_____

_____

_____

_____

_____

_____

_____

_____

_____

_____

_____

_____

_____

_____

"Light yourself on fire with passion and people will come from miles to watch you burn." – John Wesley

Day 14

Who inspired you today?
Why?
Who did you inspire?

_____

_____

_____

_____

_____

_____

_____

_____

_____

_____

_____

_____

_____

_____

"Look for a way to lift someone up. And if that's all you do, that's enough." – Elizabeth Lesser

Day 15

SOME THINGS TO THINK ABOUT...

What do you love?
Do you love yourself?
How can you bring more love into your life?

_____

_____

_____

_____

_____

_____

_____

_____

_____

_____

_____

_____

_____

_____

_____

_____

_____

_____

_____

_____

"The most important relationship you have in life is the one you have with yourself. And then after that, I'd say once you have that, it may be hard work, but you can actually design your life." – Diane von Furstenberg

Day 16

SOME THINGS TO THINK ABOUT...

What will your legacy be one day?
How do you want to make people feel?
How can you start working on that this week?

_____

_____

_____

_____

_____

_____

_____

_____

_____

_____

_____

_____

_____

_____

"The things you do for yourself are gone when you are gone, but the things you do for others remain as your legacy."
– Kalu Ndukwe Kalu

Day 17

SOME THINGS TO THINK ABOUT...

What's the biggest goal you want to achieve over the next year?
How can you approach that goal fearlessly?
What can you do this week to get started?

_____

_____

_____

_____

_____

_____

_____

_____

_____

_____

_____

_____

_____

_____

_____

_____

_____

"Just don't give up trying to do what you really want to do. Where there is love and inspiration, I don't think you can go wrong." – Ella Fitzgerald

Day 18

Is your happiness a priority for you?
In what ways do you honor your happiness?
In what ways do you devalue it?

_____

_____

_____

_____

_____

_____

_____

_____

_____

_____

_____

_____

_____

_____

_____

"I believe that happy girls are the prettiest." – Audrey Hepburn

Day 19

SOME THINGS TO THINK ABOUT...

What does your perfect day look like?
Did today come close?
If not, what can you do tomorrow to get closer?

_____

_____

_____

_____

_____

_____

_____

_____

_____

_____

_____

_____

_____

_____

_____

_____

_____

_____

"I have looked in the mirror every morning and asked myself: 'If today were the last day of my life, would I want to do what I am about to do today?' And whenever the answer has been 'No' for too many days in a row, I know I need to change something." – Steve Jobs

Day 20

What are you most proud of in your life?
Did you make yourself proud today?
Did you feel empowered today?

_____

_____

_____

_____

_____

_____

_____

_____

_____

_____

_____

_____

_____

_____

_____

_____

_____

"The most alluring thing a woman can have is confidence." – Beyonce

Day 21

SOME THINGS TO THINK ABOUT...

What, if you accomplished this week, would make you most excited?
What is the biggest change you're willing to make this week?
Imagine you just had a perfect week. What 3 things did you accomplish?

_____

_____

_____

_____

_____

_____

_____

_____

_____

_____

_____

_____

_____

_____

_____

_____

_____

"If you do what you've always done, you'll get what you've always gotten." – Tony Robbins

Day 22

SOME THINGS TO THINK ABOUT...

What would you do if you knew you couldn't fail?
How would your life change if you acted in faith vs. fear?
If you were to fully live your life, what is the first change you'd make?

_____

_____

_____

_____

_____

_____

_____

_____

_____

_____

_____

_____

_____

_____

_____

"The biggest adventure you can ever take is to live the life of your dreams." – Oprah Winfrey

Day 25

What's missing in your life right now?
What do you secretly desire?
Where does your life need the biggest upgrade?

_____

_____

_____

_____

_____

_____

_____

_____

_____

_____

_____

_____

_____

_____

_____

_____

_____

_____

_____

"I'm choosing happiness over suffering, I know I am. I'm making space for the unknown future to fill up my life with yet-to-come surprises." – Elizabeth Gilbert

Day 24

SOME THINGS TO THINK ABOUT...

If you hit the lottery, what would you do?
If money were no object, how would you spend your days?
If there were an outcome you secretly wanted, what would it be?

_____

_____

_____

_____

_____

_____

_____

_____

_____

_____

_____

_____

_____

_____

_____

_____

"You can only become truly accomplished at something you love. Don't make money your goal. Instead pursue the things you love doing and then do them so well that people can't take their eyes off of you." – Maya Angelou

Day 25

What needs to shift in order to live your dream life?
How can you focus on that shift tomorrow?
How can you focus on that shift next month?

_____

_____

_____

_____

_____

_____

_____

_____

_____

_____

_____

_____

_____

_____

_____

_____

_____

_____

"The best day of your life is the one in which you decide your life is your own. No apologies or excuses. No one to lean on, rely on, or blame. The gift is yours – it is an amazing journey – and you alone are responsible for the quality of it. This is the day your life really begins." – Bob Moawad

Day 26

SOME THINGS TO THINK ABOUT...

What 3 habits do you have that *don't* support or uplift you?
How do those habits impact your life?
What do you need to do to release them?

_____

_____

_____

_____

_____

_____

_____

_____

_____

_____

_____

_____

_____

_____

_____

"Your self-talk creates your reality. Is it time you rewired your brain and created new thoughts and habits to help bring you what you DO want as opposed to what you don't want? That voice inside your head has a huge impact on who you are and how you live your life." – Abhishek Kumar

Day 27

SOME THINGS TO THINK ABOUT...

What is your "word" for this year? (your theme)
What do you want more of in your life?
What do you want less of in your life?

_____

_____

_____

_____

_____

_____

_____

_____

_____

_____

_____

_____

_____

_____

_____

_____

_____

_____

"It is so liberating to really know what I want, what truly makes me happy, what I will not tolerate. I have learned that it is no one else's job to take care of me but me." – Beyonce

Day 28

What are you still holding on to?
How does it benefit you to hold on?
How will you benefit if you let go?

_____

_____

_____

_____

_____

_____

_____

_____

_____

_____

_____

_____

_____

_____

_____

_____

_____

"The truth is, unless you let go, unless you forgive yourself, unless you forgive the situation, unless you realize that the situation is over, you cannot move forward." – Steve Maraboli

Day 29

SOME THINGS TO THINK ABOUT...

What haven't you admitted out loud yet?
What are you avoiding?
What do you gain from staying stuck?

_____

_____

_____

_____

_____

_____

_____

_____

_____

_____

_____

_____

_____

_____

_____

_____

_____

"The most courageous act is still to think for yourself. Aloud." – Coco Chanel

Day 30

SOME THINGS TO THINK ABOUT...

Imagine for a moment you're living your dream life:
What are you saying to yourself?
What do others notice about you?
How does it feel?

_____

_____

_____

_____

_____

_____

_____

_____

_____

_____

_____

_____

_____

_____

"Tell me, what is it you plan to do with your one wild and precious life?" – Mary Oliver

NOTES

Notes & Revelations

Notes & Revelations

Notes & Revelations

Notes & Revelations

Notes & Revelations

Notes & Revelations

Notes & Revelations

Notes & Revelations

Notes & Revelations

Notes & Revelations

Notes & Revelations

Notes & Revelations

Notes & Revelations

Notes & Revelations

About Cara

Who says self-help can't be glamorous? As a bestselling and award winning author, radio host, and master life coach, Cara Alwill Leyba empowers women to live their most effervescent lives, celebrate themselves every day, and make their happiness a priority.

In the past four years, she has self-published five Amazon best selling books that have all reached #1 on various best seller categories on Amazon including Self-Help, Self-Esteem, Motivation, and Women in Business, and have gained massive popularity around the world. In July 2016, Inc. magazine named one of Cara's most recent books, *Girl Code,* one of the "Top 9 books every female entrepreneur should read" alongside *Lean In* by Sheryl Sandberg, *Thrive* by Arianna Huffington, and *#Girlboss* by Sophia Amoruso. In November 2016, *Girl Code* won a SOVA award for best audiobook in the business and education category.

Cara's chic approach to self-help has attracted thousands of women to attend her workshops and events around the country, and listen to her weekly live call-in radio show, *Slay Baby Radio.* She is often sought out by the media to help women challenge their fears and create their best lives and has been featured in *Glamour, Shape, Success, Vibe, Huffington Post, PopSugar, Cosmopolitan, Marie Claire, MSN.com* and *The Daily Mail* to name a few as well as on broadcast programs including nationally syndicated *BetterTV, Pix11 New York Morning News* on WPIX-TV, *Good Day Chicago* on WFLD-TV, *Good Day Austin* on KTBC-TV, *FOX 45 Baltimore* on WBFF-TV, *Indy Style* on WISH-TV, *CT Style* on WTNH-TV, *Oklahoma Live* on KSBI-TV and *The Women Recharged Network.* In October 2015, she was invited to be a guest speaker at the American Chamber of Commerce in Tokyo where she spoke to its members about the power of personal branding. In November 2015, Cara was named one of *YFS Magazine's* "Top 10 Women Entrepreneurs That Will Inspire You."

As a social influencer, Cara reaches her following of over 80,000 fans across all her social media platforms and inspires them daily with lifestyle tips, mindset advice, #girlboss strategies, and does it all with a chic and fashionable flair. Cara has done collaborations with Macy's, Kate Spade, SoulCycle, and others.

Follow Cara on Instagram for daily inspiration at Instagram.com/TheChampagneDiet

Learn more about Cara at www.CaraAlwill.com